MADWOMAN

MADWOMAN

SHARA McCALLUM

PEEPAL TREE

First published in Great Britain in 2017
Peepal Tree Press Ltd
17 King's Avenue
Leeds LS6 1QS
UK

Also published in the USA in 2017
by Alice James Books
114 Prescott St.
Farmington, ME 04938

ISBN 13: 9781845233396

Supported using public funding by
ARTS COUNCIL
ENGLAND

CONTENTS

ACKNOWLEDGMENTS

I extend my sincere gratitude to the editors of the following magazines and journals, in which poems in this collection first appeared, sometimes in earlier versions:

The Account, *Alaska Quarterly Review*, *The American Journal of Poetry*, *Antioch Review*, *Berkeley Poetry Review*, *Blackbox Manifold*, *Boulevard*, *The Caribbean Review of Books*, *Crazyhorse*, *The Cumberland River Review*, *Ecotone*, *Fjords Review*, *Gettysburg Review*, *Glass: A Journal of Poetry*, *Great River Review*, *Guernica*, *Kenyon Review*, *The Massachusetts Review*, *MiPOesias*, *Moko*, *Pleiades*, *Poetry Northwest*, *The Southern Review*, *Stand*.

"Lucea, Jamaica", "Madwoman as Salome", "Madwoman Exiled", "Madwoman in Middle Age", "Manchineel", "The Story of Madwoman and Horse", "The Story of Madwoman and River Mumma", and "West Coast" appeared, sometimes in earlier versions, in the "New Poems" section of *The Face of Water: New and Selected Poems* (Peepal Tree Press, 2011) and are reprinted with permission of the press; "Fury" appeared in *This Strange Land* (Alice James Books, 2011) and is reprinted with permission of the press; "Memory", "Hour of Duppy and Dream", "The Parable of the Wayward Child", and "Now I'm a Mother" were reprinted by the online journal, *Shining Rock Poetry Anthology & Book Review* (Spring 2016); "The Dream" was featured online at *Poetry Daily* (February 28, 2015); "Parasol" was reprinted in *Best American Poetry 2014* (Scribner, 2014).

For fellowships which aided in the writing of these poems, I wish to thank the National Endowment for the Arts and the U.S. Poet Laureate Natasha Trethewey, the Witter Bynner Foundation, and the Poetry and Literature Center at the Library of Congress.

For their love and belief in me, I am grateful as always for my husband Steven Shwartzer, our daughters Rachel and Naomi, and my other family members and friends. Poets whose friendship and example sustain me are too numerous to name here, but I offer special thanks to Paula Closson Buck, Terrance Hayes, and Mia Leonin for their generous readings of this manuscript. Tremendous thanks, for the gift of their faith, to Jeremy Poynting, Kwame Dawes, Hannah Bannister, and everyone connected with Peepal Tree.

For Steve, Rachel, & Naomi

&

In memory of my grandparents:

Sally Kathleen Norris DePass (1932-2014)

David Leslie DePass (1934-2012)

Memory is the only
afterlife I can understand...

— Lisel Mueller

LITTLE SOUL
after Hadrian

Little soul – kind, wandering –
body's host and guest,

look how you've lowered yourself,
moving in a world of ice,

washed of colour. My girl,
what compelled you once

is no more.

*

MEMORY

I bruise the way the most secreted,
most tender part of a thigh exposed
purples then blues. No spit-shine shoes,
I'm dirt you can't wash from your feet.
Wherever you go, know I'm the wind
accosting the trees, the howling night
of your sea. Try to leave me, I'll pin you
between a rock and a hard place, will hunt you,
even as you erase your tracks
with the tail-ends of your skirt. You think
I'm gristle, begging to be chewed?
No, my love: I'm bone. Rather: the sound
bone makes when it snaps; that ditty
lingering in you, like ruin.

TO RED

I've been wrong about you so long.
You're not the colour of war
on Kingston streets. When you stain
you become rust. You cheat
even the flame tree, more orange
in truth than you in your crimson,
your scarlet robes. Not even
the poppy contains you.
Not even one hundred huddled
in the field. Maybe
like you I am a liar. Or memory
is a story I keep telling myself.
But I understand, being as you are
from a long line of women
who regard facts as suggestion,
who know what it is to burn
inside the closet of night.
Which is why when I reach for you
and you careen, the nearer you come
to my yellow, my alabaster skin,
I still croon your name.
I still insist on you, my lovely,
my death, my life.

RACE

You are the original incognito.
Transparent, all things shine through you.
She's the whitest black girl you ever saw,
lighter than "flesh" in the Crayola box.
But, man, look at that ass and look at her shake it
were just words, not sticks or stones, flung
when dresses were the proof that clung like skin,
when lipstick stained brighter than any blood.
Girl, who is it now you'd want to see you?
And what would that mean: *to be seen*?
Why not make a blessing of what
all these years you've thought a curse?
You are so everywhere, so nowhere;
in plain sight you walk through walls.

MADWOMAN AS SALOME

Back then I was a character in my own life,
daily imagining the possible.

I could be a small pea, clasped
in a fist, or offer my body —

veiled, masking
its multiple skins.

How did I come to stand
in an abrasion of light?

How did I find myself
undressing for others, pivoting

to capture any gaze, fasten it
onto my flesh?

Love, if you had seen me when
I was that girl,

would you have recognised me
or turned your face away?

THE PARABLE OF THE WAYWARD CHILD

Yu know how yu can see car careening
before it even start accelerate? Is same
with she. In the crib she bawl, she bawl
till she cyan done. All her life, as if
she in a race with ruin. I know I wasting
mi breath fi hope one day she go realise
wanting nuh mek yu special. Even I –
who cotch-up miself on the side a precipice
one time and was schupid enough
fi think it a place fi set up shop –
did wake-up quick-quick once mi foot slip.
When edge draw near fi true
only a fool nuh accept the idea of falling
plenty-plenty different from the drop.

VESTA TO MADWOMAN

Was a time I thought to extinguish flames,
but blue tongues licked at the edges of sleep,

waking me to strike that first match.
So, yes, I was an arsonist.

But have you considered destruction
is kin to desire?

The ruined and those that ruin
require each other, the way fire

needs oxygen to light. A blaze
razes a field without thought and, I admit,

sometimes you were that field.
But, my girl, look what this has sown in you:

to know what is sifted from ash
is lit by the embers of disaster.

MADWOMAN'S GEOGRAPHY

In my first life, I slid
into the length of a snake. Then

sloughed scales for wings.
Was content one hundred years

till the air, as all things must,
lost its charms. After a long time

falling, I landed in the sea.
What could I do but follow

any wake? How else chart
a course than the way a child

plucks flowers from a field —
the eye compelling the hand to reach?

THE STORY OF MADWOMAN AND IXORA

she plucked the red flowers from the bush in the garden
      where tamarinds were strewn and rotting underfoot   she waded
a sovereign or a god   feeling little remorse for wreckage wrought by whim

      these flowers were bystanders   in the daily drama   she enacted
to combat boredom
           so perhaps hers was an act of cruelty

but she was a child   and whatever eddied around her
               rafted inside the certainty

      that as these flowers returned each morning
seemingly waiting for her outstretched hand
           so day would follow night

she was a child
       and did not conceive of beauty
    as something that could end   or

      in memory   become unbearable

EXILE

Say *morning,*
        and a bird trills on a doorstep
                outside a kitchen.

Inside, fingers roll johnnycakes,
        dropping balls of dough into oil,
                splattering, singeing a wrist.

Here, a woman is always
        singing, each note tethering
                sound to meaning.

The trick is to wait
        on this doorstep forever.
                The trick is to remember

time is a fish
        swimming through dark water.

LUCEA, JAMAICA

at the Hanover Infirmary, 1996

What I saw there I could not carry.
She'd lifted a sheet, revealing her abscess.
I was a young woman then,
travelling toward some notion of home.

But a sheet had been lifted, an abscess revealed.
I'd hoped I might meet myself,
travelled home with some notion
of finding the girl I was in braids.

I'd hoped to meet this younger self
on a coastal road bridging towns,
but another girl with braided hair
waved each morning I arrived.

A crossroad between tourist towns,
Lucea is a place you could miss.
Arriving each morning, I thought
if I looked long enough I'd find

not an idea but the place itself.
Coming to a part of my country I didn't know,
I looked long to find –
liquid pools in opened flesh.

Coming to a country I thought I knew –
a young woman,
liquid and open-fleshed –
I saw there what I could not carry.

JOURNEYING TO BLACK RIVER

At the mouth, flooded with brackish water,
a crocodile suns on the bank,
till with a start it wakes and slips in,
swimming toward the boat,
nearly reaching the side before submerging.
Mangroves grow on this river's shores,
roots shooting down, while up in branches
egrets roost, hundreds of them unmoving
as we slide along, Santa Cruz range
falling to the Pedro Plain, Cockpit Country
ahead, this land cleaved
by the river, this place where past
and present collide, and I too
am runnelled. I too am riven.

HISTORY AND MYTH

This was the most beautiful land that eye could behold...
— Christopher Columbus

The way mist shrouds mountains

Long ago I learned a lesson

salt roils inland from sea

in etymology

Nanny roams Cockpit Country

Xaymaca Arawak land of wood and water

Nanny leader of the Maroons

Santiago Spanish patron saint

mystifying the British

Jamaica brined in English

bouncing bullets off her backside

Long ago

refusing a treaty that would

I was made to understand

barter one's freedom for another's

history

Nanny like the goat so-named

is a word

that will not cease bleating

THE STORY OF MADWOMAN AND HORSE

when the horse came to the window her master yanked her back
but in that moment she had seen through nearly opaque glass the
creature their eyes meeting inside the pane's reflection not one
adult looked up from her hand of cards or stopped drinking his
gin not one could anticipate the whip cutting through night air or
feel the sting of blows landing on her back not one heard her cries
carried by the railing wind when she was sent to bed and the
darkness enfolded her then feet beneath sheets she galloped
across fields

WEST COAST

for Dora Sandybird & for my grandmother

> *...there never was a world for her*
> *Except the one she sang and, singing, made.*
> —Wallace Stevens

Hello darling, she calls,
leaning over a wooden railing,
in lilac dress and grey, knitted cap,
framed by morning light, an open
door. Perched on her porch,
gaze absent, she seems waiting
for someone to enter her view.
Then eyes snap into focus,
an arm extends in greeting.
She descends cement blocks
doubling as stairs, with speed
and grace belying her age.
Her body become
a taut line of longing.

*

Docked in her yard on empty oil drums,
a fifteen-foot fishing boat
almost eclipses her face,
her house, the whole of this scene.
Trellising the keel, weeds sprout
lavender flowers. A vine froths
white stars. Another, maybe pumpkin,
wraps and climbs, entering the hull.
The wood is rotting,
paint faded and chipped,
but *West Coast*, stencilled
on the starboard side, remains legible,

reminding all who pass this way
exactly where we are.

*

A mind adrift in memory,
she repeats phrases each time we meet:
My father was a fisherman, you know?
I had my swim already.
Mr. Stevens, on some matters
we can agree: there is no world
for her but this one she makes.
Yet about the sea, I fear
you were wrong: no one gets to sing
beyond its genius. Original mystery,
the sea closes itself to scrutiny
like pods my daughters collect
on its shores. They rattle, but when
split open no seeds spill into our hands.

*

This time of day the sun
is a mound of butter, arranged
on a bone china plate.
Past her house, a narrow path
leads down a hill of bougainvillea,
desert rose and frangipani, blooms
strewn across rocky ground.
Then soil turns to sand, a clearing
opens, delivering me
to the sea. Each morning
I run its shoreline, testing tides
and my body's limits – her voice
the chorus I cannot outdistance:
Alright darling. You go.

PARASOL

You could still become a queen.
When, a slip of a girl,

you directed trees
to lower their limbs,

neither fire ants nor sap
could stop your climb,

nor rain that lightly fell,
misting leaves.

Inside a story's spell,
you find your way back

where a stone on a path waits
for you to stumble.

Like the kaleidoscope's contents,
time is jumbled, opening at will.

Now: a too-bright sun and you,
teetering on a wall,

parasol clutched tight as you tumble.
This parasol is, for a moment,

everything you've lost
and all that can console.

MADWOMAN IN MIDDLE AGE

As a girl, I knew the world as mutable.
A beggar could pass for king,

a maiden morph into a fish.
When the caterpillar's husk unfolded

as wings, I believed even the dead
could be returned. I walked across

a sea and then an ocean. For years
I flaked their remnants off my skin,

flung them over my shoulder to shake
the old people's prophecy:

All her life
that gal going suck salt.

In a new country I became
a woman, mistaking

what I'd loved for what I'd lost.
Now I tell myself

every red is not a shade
meant to shame a poppy.

Now when tea leaves drift
through steaming water,

sifting into shape, I say:
This portends nothing.

CODA

Still. I call back

    the air —
        in early morning misted
            midday so hot
                a body would pine for wind

    the sound of hens
pecking ground
            moments after corn left my hands
                    scattering

and when —
        the goat bound and bleating —
      I became that animal
           and the one who inflicted its wound

FURY

The madwoman wanders the hall of mirrors. The parrot perched on her shoulder squawks, *Again. Again,* its mantra heeded by no one. The madwoman counts minutes, sees patience as a ticking out of life's losses. In her fingers, she briefly holds each memory before letting her hands fall back at her sides. Now she is no longer a girl running in a garden saturated with lemon trees. She thinks this morning she might be the parrot mimicking language. Or perhaps she has become the single word delivered from its maw.

In the country where she lives, which is no country, the madwoman maps desire's coordinates onto her body. Each hand pressing into her back meets the others that have lingered in that spot; each lover tastes the breath of those gone before, ghosting in her kisses – the madwoman now being all women. The hysteric who cordons off danger so others can believe in safety. The anorectic who starves her flesh so others may eat. The whore whose sex blooms thorns. The mystic whose dust-covered feet discredit her visions. The mother whose placid gaze masks the storm gathering fury into its centre.

HOUR OF DUPPY AND DREAM

All my life I have been pursued by whispers —
What pickney so greedy it consume its own mumma?

I was born at the time of day between night
and morning, the hour of duppy and dream.

My mother's screams seamed the world I left
and the one I entered, her spirit extinguished

the instant mine lit. Before consciousness
took hold, I knew my life would be marked

by her sorrow, pressed into my skin;
by her laughter, broken stones that fill my mouth.

Now, when wind gathers at the hem of dawn,
I listen for her wail rattling through cane

to recall: no one asks for the meal
that leaves us hungry. Yet we eat.

NOW I'M A MOTHER

What does the world look like? *Sublime?* you ask, now I'm a mother.
Sometimes. But, thing is, I also suck limes now I'm a mother.

Watch me whirl, a spinning top, kaleidoscopic universe of *hurry*.
Always in a flurry, I'm anxiety's mime now I'm a mother.

Everything I've said and done has come back to bite me in the ass.
Humility's what I'm learning – time after time – now I'm a mother.

You hear the same lament on talk shows, in self-help books, at water coolers:
I was too blind/young/foolish to see. I was in my prime. Now I'm a mother.

My friend expounds: *Each of you are remote* – a theory based on his own mother.
I can't help wondering: is loneliness my crime now I'm a mother?

In the end, I couldn't keep up the charade: my child figured out I was no God.
What a relief! It was exhausting, perfection's climb. Now I'm a mother.

Nothing about it is sublime? you try again. Younger version of me, take heart:
of course there are days that chime a perfect rhyme now I'm a mother.

My real name's Dispenser-of-Band-Aids but call me *Earth*, if you would rather.
It's all the same to me. Even *Shara* is just a pseudonym now I'm a mother.

THE DEER

after Franz Marc's Deer in the Forest, I, 1913

A study in panic: this doe and fawn,
stilled by your car rounding a bend.
In Marc's painting, deer curl
into one another. A swirl
of birds and gestural trees
enclose them in a fairy-tale-like thicket.
So unlike your neighbourhood, where
they wander yards, chew up gardens,
dart blindly into roads, where
these two, stunted by fear,
don't know to go forward or retreat.
What should we do?
asks the voice from the back seat.
And you have no good reply.
In Marc's painting, the deer become
the war that took his life or
are its opposite: death kept on a leash
by the canvas's frame. But these deer
in front of you are not
playthings of the imagination,
these two blocking your path
are real. And until they behave as deer
will and flee – you are all stranded.

MANCHINEEL

We lived in the house of the slamming doors, wind blowing into and through each room, turning the whole of it into a raft, billowing curtains like sails, setting the four of us adrift. Daily we took the footpath to the sea, the children collecting rocks, picking weeds they insisted were flowers, sidestepping the plague of snails, entrails splayed in the sun.

Once wandering the Flower Forest, they braceletted their arms and wrists with millipedes. As if in a dream, we saw and smiled. Only when their fingertips flared did we remember we'd been given warnings to heed: *Avoid the manchineel tree, its poison apples, its leaves weeping skin-blistering sap after rain.*

Days were spent with each of us bound to repetition: trawling market stalls for fruit, stealing from and returning to the sea its trinkets. Trudging uphill when the sky flushed pink and indigo and, on again arriving home, scooping frogs that kept marooning themselves
in our pool.

STUDY OF A GRASSHOPPER

At dusk, voices of children playing,
then crying when called home,
invade. You collage such scraps,
these sounds you title: *My children*
will grow up to leave. You believe
small losses tally up and note stones
underfoot. Overhead, migrating birds'
queued bodies appear like smoke
on a backdrop of red. Before
their retreat is complete, you think,
We are temporary. A grasshopper
hurdles about your legs, and your child
dashes around the yard, her limbs
blurred by intention: to catch fireflies
that will light her hands. And in a flash
you exchange your daughter,
on her chase, for the passage of time or
the way the future will disappoint her.
This is a pitfall of metaphor: so quickly
it displaces what's in front of us. Now
the grasshopper hopping madly nearby
recaptures your attention, and your mind
makes that same leaping motion,
turning the insect into your own restlessness.

MOTHER LOVE, A BLUES

My mother hung laundry on the line,
sheets and our small clothes clipped with pins.
Sometimes she gave us castor oil with juice.
Sometimes we left for school in unshined shoes.

My mother hung laundry on the line,
the sun doing its work of drying,
sometimes in minutes, as we circled the yard.
Sometimes porridge was boiling on the stove.

My mother hung laundry on the line,
young and what some called beautiful:
blonde hair – an aura, a mane, or a flame –
often, when she wept, curtaining her face.

My mother strung what, exactly,
to that line? Older than she was then,
what do I know anymore to be true,
what do I invent? My mother

hung laundry on a line – every day
or once in my whole childhood?
Sometimes she loved us. Sometimes herself.
Often it was neither, or both.

THE PARABLE OF JOHN CROW

Is not one John Crow shit on her head,
was a whole flock. Long time
I try to puzzle out how she, who did shine
pretty-pretty, brighter than the moon own self,
could lose all she shimmer like so.
She turn so wutless (a so them say).
She mad fi rass (a so them say).
Look how she mash-up everything she touch.
Now, I come to think is all a we blind
to what she mussa know. Nuh true:
one day the wind a come fi each a we
and knock we down? Nuh true when yu let go
the deggy-deggy branch yu cling to –
courage or not, yu haffi meet yuself at last.

THE STORY OF MADWOMAN AND RIVER MUMMA

stepping across algae-covered rocks that moonless night she lost her
perch and fell into the river not knowing how to swim she did not
panic at first *surely not only fish can breathe underwater* the thought came
to her but on its heels memory of land and air quickly followed
pressing their weight into her lungs hands reached up to grip her
then cracking the river's skin she came up sputtering that night and
since she has stood on many a riverbank at the edge of many a sea
staring into the face of water to be made again to believe

TEN THINGS YOU MIGHT LIKE TO KNOW ABOUT MADWOMAN

1. The source of her rage and joy are the same, which is true of many people where she's from, who, at one point or another, have not had a pot to piss in.

2. Like everyone, she has her flaws. For instance: she's convinced of the importance of her own grief.

3. In her own mind, she sometimes moonlights as the earth. As a girl she once built a raft from blue mahoe, masking tape, and her own foolishness.

3b. This may or may not be true, but sharks wouldn't go near it anyway.

4. For instance: she really loves Abba and thinks "Chiquitita" was written for her, personally. If you know the song, or might care to google it and listen on YouTube, even if you don't understand why she persists in this delusion, she hopes — despite your better judgment, taste in music, and/or profound sense of ironic detachment — that you'll love it.

5. While she has little actual faith (having lost most of it some-where in a gully, perhaps in a big rainstorm that took place sometime in her childhood, which is her usual guess for every-thing) and therefore cannot in good conscience recommend to you the act of praying, she has nonetheless cultivated a deep belief in the colour red — as in the poppy, which she admires since it seems harnessed to nothing but its own fiery display.

7½. She has already grown tired of this list and is irritated (with herself, not you) that she is now obligated to four or five more disclosures, depending on how you're counting.

6. She is concerned details of her past make people uncomfortable. For example: her father was crazy, and not just in the colloquial sense. For example: he killed himself.

5b. *It might be better to be a gardenia. Less showy.* This is what she thinks on the days she's not admiring the poppy.

6b. Since she's told you this story of her father, she wants to assure you she's fine now, which you might conclude anyway, if you met her, because she smiles a lot.

7. She has problems distinguishing fact from fiction.

8. Also, she's concerned lists are way too postmodern, a theory, which at first she thinks is shiny as a new penny, then quickly finds annoying and infectious, like sand flies. She wants to assure you this is true even if she is mixed-race, from a host of nations, the sum of a bunch of world religions, and born in 1972.

8b. Now that she's alluded to literature and theory, she's a bit alarmed you might begin to think of her as a character in a story. On the other hand, she likes stories very much, especially those rarer ones in which women get to be the heroes, so if you can't help yourself, then she thinks it would be okay, but asks that you please make her a myth.

5c. *Or would it be better to be a cricket?* she wonders. She's primarily thinking of the chirping kind when she asks herself this, but if your brain hears "cricket" and jumps to the sport then items # 1, 3, 4, and 5 will likely carry different meaning for you.

9. She's pleased the numerical value of the Hebrew word *chai* (meaning "life") is 18 because she happens to have been born on October 18th. She's always liked coincidences, like this one, or that her name means "poetry" and "song" (Hebrew again), or that she emigrated from Jamaica to the US on the day of Bob Marley's

funeral. She thinks 18 must therefore be an omen, which is useful because, even if she doesn't believe in signs, this gives her an exit strategy. And she's always heard it's a good idea to quit while you're ahead (presuming you're ahead).

10. Okay, now she's concerned that last item was too hopeful, too perfect, or was trying too hard: all of the above, or none of them, she can't quite put her finger on it.

10b. But, more importantly, she's worried that, if you've been paying attention, you've likely figured out she's confused about many things. For example: math, God, the hegemony of ice cream over all other desserts, memory, parental love, her defence of wearing dresses in winter, all endings but notably those of poems and people, winter itself, all other types of love, the universe, origins, eternity, and so on.

SHE

She could sing the blue out of water
She could sing the meat off a bone
She could sing the fire out of burning
She could sing a body out of home

She could sing the eye out of a hurricane
She could sing the fox right out its hole
She could sing the devil from the details
She could sing the lonely from a soul

She could sing a lesson in a yardstick
She could sing the duppy out of night
She could sing the shoeless out of homesick
She could sing a wrong out of a right

She could sing the prickle from the nettle
She could sing the sorrow out of stone
She could sing the tender from the bitter
She could sing the never out of gone

THE PARABLE OF SHIT AND FLOWERS

I not the Lord. If I turn the other cheek,
is mi ass them going get. Yu? From time
yu was lickle bit, yu pick up one ugly bug
and call it beautiful. Yu stop fi chat
with every sore-foot man in the street.
Even how yu is big woman, come in like yu forget
what people can do. Gal, yu too trusting.
I did tell yu that long time but I see now
yu hard-a-hearing. Yu ignorant so till mi nuh know
what to do with yu. Yu don't even watch news –
stick yu head in sand like ostrich. Child,
life no easy, fi true. Yu choose fi believe
is only bed a rose, but hear mi: I did grow them.
And what yu haffi put in dirt stink to rass,
but is what mek them come up.

WHY MADWOMAN SHOULDN'T READ THE NEWS

I know you'll say I'm overreacting,
but my mother's prophesying has come to pass:
Armageddon is upon us. Just look at the evidence:
the carriers of our species at every second
being raped and killed and the rare ones
who survive offing their lovers and children
(or worse, if it can be believed, wearing bangs),
molesters and gun-toters skulking
in every lunchbox, the environment
churning into apocalypse. Oh, kids,
please save us the heartache and leave
in advance; calmly but quickly
abandon your seesaws and swings. Friends,
do you remember when we were young?
Life plump with promise and dreams?
Me neither. Anyway, who'd be naive enough
now to believe in anything so impossible-
to-attain as happiness or justice? Sure
we had a run of it. Even some laughs.
But the day's arrived, as deep down we knew
it would, and spectacles streaming
from across the globe should convince
even the most sceptical
of our soon-to-be extinction.
Not that we listen to true madmen
anymore, but the older I get
the more certain I become: my father
would have been heralded a prophet
had he lived, would have joined his brethren
and sistren on every street corner, trumpeting
this end from the beginning.

MADWOMAN TO HER DELIVERER

In you and me resides a history of faith.
Yours in freedom delivered with a gun.

Mine in the fable of moon and sun
meeting at dusk and dawn. Though now

I see I have always been for you
a smattering of stars you fix

in your gaze, a constellation you view
as a distant notion. My love,

how much longer can you carry on,
renaming destruction *rescue* and *peace*?

For how many more centuries
do you imagine I can excavate

the part of you that does not issue orders
from the part that follows them?

THE STORY OF MADWOMAN AND COCKROACH

One day she woke to find a roach perched on her nose. Outside the house in which she slept the sun had been making itself felt for hours and had been creeping into her room through the left-open jalousies. But not until the creature flew through the window and landed on her face did she stir.

Perhaps this was the moment in her small life when she came closest to being undone by what she feared. Perhaps she saw the animal as herself, considered for the first time that it existed, as she did, without knowing why.

A child awakened with a start might lament the loss of her unfinished dream, its fragments fading but lodging like shrapnel inside of her. Or she might regard herself as lucky, having been ferried safely from the world of the dead back to that of the waking.

Had she had the time or the wisdom to weigh these choices in the instant the roach alighted, she might have flicked it away, watched it scurry into a crevice in the wall or into the shadows under her bed. But startled, instead she grabbed the insect. And screaming a scream that continues to this day, she crushed it.

RUNNING

Stone wall that replaced sand in this cove
waited for your feet to navigate it, as the man who drove

beside you – girl in plaits, in your uniform with pleats –
waited, slowing to a crawl to call, *Little sister, please,*

adding, *Psst-psst-psst*, that sound some men make,
that lisping to make you look, to direct your gaze,

as the man in this inlet waited to piss, straddling the path,
splaying a sickle-toothed grin as now you swerve past,

thinking – *Motherfucker* –
but rendered mute only run faster,

not chancing a glance behind to see the sun
draining the sky of colour, the sun slung low on the horizon

at this hour, this hour reprising every twilight
in you, in you every falling again into night.

MADWOMAN EXILED

Walking from the house of my earliest dreams,
I pass the field where I collected cerasee

to boil into tea, pass my birth tree, its roots
and my umbilical cord entwined.

Next town I enter, I will kneel
on the steps of the first church I find,

plant myself in the path of parishioners
who turn from me, tipping their faces

to a blistering sky. Day upon day,
I will sink my hair into a pail.

Whore of Babylon, Abomination, I
will take matted strands to stone,

scouring, for all who must see to see,
the scourge he left in me.

MADWOMAN AS RASTA MEDUSA

I-woman go turn all a Babylon to stone.
I-woman is the Deliverer and the Truth.
Look pon I and feel yu inside calcify.
Look pon I and witness the chasm,
the abyss of yuself rupture. Look pon I
and know what bring destruction.
Yu say I-woman is monstrosity
but is yu gravalicious ways
mek I come the way I come.
Is yu belief everyone exist fi satisfy
yu wanton wantonness.
Yu think, all these years gone,
I-woman a come here fi revenge.
Wo-yo — but is wrong again yu wrong.
I-woman is the Reckoning and Judgement Day.
This face, etch with wretchedness,
these dreads, writhing and hissing
misery, is not the Terror.
I-woman is what birth from yu Terror.

OH ABUSE

When I try to locate you, I think maybe
you are lodged in my scapula like ill-formed wings.
When I listen for your voice, I hear a faint
lullaby of razors and knives, though fainter.
You are my first darkness, but I continue
wanting to see you as a sapling, greening
and tendrilling. I am perhaps naive enough
to believe, if I could unlock your origin,
I would glean knowledge of what separates a spirit
from itself, would understand what makes each of us
sometimes that creature of no-good, of pure
wutlessness. Oh abuse, you swallowed the sun
when you came but also taught me
it never shines for any of us, exactly –
a gift I have thanked you for many a time since.
So, no, I am not calling you to account for your sins.
What use would that be to either of us, travellers,
landed so far from where we began?
No, I am asking you to step into the light
so I may finally behold your face or, please,
when I speak the only name for you I have,
please, just once, answer.

SALOME TO MADWOMAN

Now I am become death, the destroyer of worlds.
———Bhagavad Gita

You too could learn what the wind
becomes when it scythes the palm. A storm
is an opportunity for all to be given
form. For every crawling and flying
creature to shift into its true shape: carcass
of bird, mongoose, bat, left to rot
in sun after. A storm is not a mirror
held for the wrongdoer's gaze but a fury
sounding its ineffable name. In the centre
of your life, you baptise
as sadness what rage has wrought.
You find absolution, calling me
Executioner. But woman,
listen now carefully: I saw myself,
never more clearly, than in the glint of steel
when I brought down that blade.

MADWOMAN TO CLAUDETTE COLVIN

Let's face it, girl, if only
      you'd acted like a lady (*Not a whore*,
            the tongues start wagging), if only

you'd pirouetted in the right circles,
      looked the part for the role (*Mercy,*
            what a shame, the tongues are now clucking),

if only you'd been older, married (*At least*
      had kept her legs shut, the heads start shaking) –
            they might have claimed you,

fashioned you,
      martyred you, sainted you.
            Oh girl (*If only, if only,*

the heads are still and always shaking),
      then, and only then,
            they might have let you play it.

LOT'S WIFE TO MADWOMAN

Like everyone else yu going get tired a mi.
As happen to all a we, my life been reduce
to one sad, tawdry cliché. Gal, just
lef mi in peace where yu find mi.
Mi never trouble miself with other vultures
who come before. Why yu fancy
yu special? Oh, yu favour mi more
yu say, with yu whole self twist-up,
twist-up with regret. Lawd, how you come
so fool-fool? So big and boasy
to presume yu can fling yuself
inna anyone story yu choose. Yu feel sey
this is play, ee? Then yu mussa forget
the crucial part: I turned to salt.

ODE TO THE APPLE

I won't linger over your fall from grace,
your myth tainted by the facts.
If anything, it was a pomegranate,

not you, hanging in that garden. Instead,
I'll extol the virtue of your latest hoodwink act:
spliced and grafted, you replicate hunger

perfected. No surprise,
when I bite your flesh I detect
the perfumed rose, another we've lassoed

to desire. No surprise, fearing our own
rotting, we wax your skin – its sheen
rivalling this dying star we orbit.

Maybe my father was merciful when
he peeled and sliced you open,
rendering you more palatable on a plate.

Oh, but that was some time ago,
and I've since grown a taste for tart, for bitter
lacing every sweet. And you

could never deliver the kind of freedom
I've long been after – to have no need
to make an Eden of this world, or any other.

ELEGY

First you told me:
Let's not cross that bridge till we come to it.

But tumours bloomed in you the way a hawk plucks prey –
without conscience or malice.

Then you said: *What to do?*
Every way yu turn makka juk yu.

And your body's betrayals grew abundant:
face bloated as a puffer fish, legs dangling like a marionette's.

Then you said: *Every day a fishing day,*
but is not every day yu ketch fish.

And I asked myself: who, if I could,
would I follow into the world of the dead?

Which was the wrong question.
Whose answer I already knew.

At the time, I believed love meant
I could not not-look. Now,

I am sure of little but death is like an ill-fitted suit
that can be worn longer than we'd imagine.

DEATH

Oh my sweet one, night doesn't call me
to roost inside your head, to fill
these small hours with my cawings.
As with all things, I am possessed
of a will wholly my own. So
you endure me by enduring,
so morning comes again, cruelly
shining its face. If these words chafe,
first hear me out, for I am in you
as the river is inside the stone.
This truth you turn from has been
your companion from the start. Oh
my sweet, you will remember me,
anytime now, despite yourself.

FABLE

You shrugged off the raiment of the living
    and I knew I would forget you,
        the way all the dead are forgotten,
    becoming an archipelago
reconstructed in dream.

And so it was your name in our mouths
    became a prayer uttered
        in a strange tongue, a snake
    swallowing its own tail, an island circled
by a ship without port.

And so it was the mountains
    came down to meet the sea
        and grew wings. And your going
    tore green from every leaf of every tree.
And the sun could find no habitation.

ELEGY BLUES

You prickling as the thornbush, you
clouds effacing the sun, you
dogging me like the casuarina
flogs the wind, you
so long, so gone, no more
see-you-later-alligator, you
not *in-a-while-crocodile*, you
not now, not ever, you
now never.

YOU

You bring out the ragged in me.
The razor-edged, cellophaned, jagged in me.

You bring out the neurotic in me.
Hours scouring for more news of ISIS in me.

You bring out the panic in me.
Never-going-to-sleep-can't-face-the-dark rising in me.

You bring out the liar in me.
I'm fine. How are you doing? rebounder in me.

You bring out the amnesic in me.
Memory, a flock of birds wheeling in me.

You bring out the bean counter in me.
Seconds measured like spoons of salt spilling in me.

You bring out the rivers in me.
And the seas and the oceans eroding in me.

You bring out the groveller in me.
The beggar, deal-maker, tightrope walker in me.

You bring out the bad music in me.
The not-so-pretty, far-from-gritty, self-pitying me.

You bring out the clouds collecting in me.
All but cumulus, the kind my child's forgotten in me.

You bring out the sorriest of Bad Wolves in me.
Dropped baskets, loose teeth, lost pathways in me.

THE DREAM

after Chagall and for Steve

In a house that is not a house
but a boat set sailing
in a landscape where darkened clouds and hills
merge and an angel hovers and a rooster
like a sentinel guards,
or inside that house where a man consoles a woman
standing next to the bed where she sits,
a vase of flowers on the table at their side,
love, find us. And find us
inside the farmhouse we rented
which all winter let in cold and mice
through cracks in its stone,
where across the field outside our window
deer trekked leaving tracks in snow
as lying in bed we watched.
If love is not this dream of itself
then it must be a waking to this dream.
If it is not a place in time
then it must be the action of placing
a vase of flowers deliberately
on a table inside a square of light.

SWEETHEART,

wind swells a horn with sound,
the way you find your way
inside me, the way your tongue
names my sorrow
                    Even now,
I'd play the fool
if you would trace your fingers
across my loneliest bones, if you would
walk with me, inside my shadow.

SORROW

There are too many poems on the subject of sorrow.
Why pile one more on this dung heap of sorrow?

Once upon a time always promises wonder. We remember,
too late, the breadcrumb-less woods of sorrow.

You fall asleep nightly rehearsing a lie:
Tomorrow I'll end it, my love affair with sorrow.

A woman is singing again. Who is she this time?
No matter. Her voice grinds the whetstone of sorrow.

What a choice we're given: to hold on to the dead
or let them vanish to try to vanquish our sorrow.

I speak my name out loud into my shiny new iPhone.
On the screen, Siri spells it out for me: *Sorrow*.

INSOMNIA

This night without end, you tune your ear
to the sounds of breathing, wind creaking
through trees, this house shuffling its feet.
Lightning stutters on bedroom walls
and to no one you say: *This is living.*
And to your other self, as if strained
through a sieve, you whisper: *Is this living?*
Please I need to know what,
in the next part of my life,
are the lessons I am meant to learn.
Dear one, why do you assume
there are lessons? Thunder cracks open
this night, in which the soul is a carpetbag,
dragged through the dimly lit streets of the body.

I
fragments and definitions

Like smoke or cinders, fire transfigured.

The voice that fidgets and refuses a chair.

Sad, sad, sad – all the while now.

Like looking up into the pear tree and receiving a fractal sky.

The zigzagging around the room.

The confusion that's just begun.

Like rockstone, stubborn and mad enough to hold on to being wronged.

Shadow boxer.

One eye blue, one brown, back turned on this town.

Like the song of the flimflam.

Sometimes subterranean. Sometimes chameleon.

The body's sparrowing out. Or the body as both lantern and shipwrecked form.

Like the kaleidoscope, reconsidered. A trick of light.

Everything misheard, misremembered.

The one-one cocoa, still trying to fill a basket with a hole.

Like moorings that don't release.

INVENTION

When I arrived, did bells ring at the Abbey of Our Lady of Exile?
Or is memory a habitual liar, craving invention after invention?

Oh the monkey business of it all, the hullabalooing of the mind,
smug and swinging with the acrobatics of its inventions.

Directionless, I travel to the farthest edges of myself,
cultivating wilderness as if it were an invention.

Even if smoke and mirrors, the beloved remains the rage.
Love, how do I go on being your marvellous invention?

If I sometimes misplace myself, who really can I blame?
The country of loss was my miscalculated invention.

Despite evidence to the contrary, I continue believing in myth.
Shara, you are the most fleeting of my inventions.

HYDE PARK

Into the park
of the ducks and swans swimming
into the laden fields
bringing in late the flowers
into the rows of roses thick with their sickly scent
over the course of hours
over the course of days
over the course of months that made a course for me
and that course became a path where
into the park I went and went as one descends
into the ruts of the mind and into
the furrows of grief leading labyrinthian back to
the grief of which there is no
naming no way out of no other utterance but
you you you
the saying of which unsays me

GRIEF

I linger, rearranging the furniture,
making the sky contract
till it no longer contains the horizon.
When I hover, you hear cicadas crescendo.
You mistake me for winter's onset
or the body as it ages. Foolish girl.
You console yourself with fables
where straw is spun to gold
yet a promise remains unpaid.
Have you really not yet learned?
Only in fairy tales is disaster averted
with a secret word. In this world,
magic claims no dominion.
Death is a door, which keeps opening.

MADWOMAN APOCRYPHA

When comes the night that made you?

                    In this field: snow not yet underfoot,
    trees whose branches are shorn of leaves,
            this sky a grey slate over and around
        houses echoing the shape of the river,

Q: What created you?
A: A breach in the self.

                  they descend –
      a swirl of smoke,
          reassembling on the grass
                  as a flock of black birds.

When comes the night of your unmaking?

             If this is the story of the mind, ferrying,
      I am standing at the edge of some larger darkness:
          bullfrog croaking, dusk falling into winter,
  oncoming night cloaking first reeds then trees,

Q: What caused the breach?
A: I'd become mistrustful of beauty again.

        each sound perforating the moment,
          casting itself as a line across water.

                *

When comes the night that made you?

Q: How do you measure the distance between
the girl you were and the woman you've become?

A: As I learned from her long ago,
with the riddle of the lemon, the answer is always one.

In Port-of-Spain I walked the Savannah, half-
expecting to see the photograph of her take form:
an English girl dressed as an Arabian Princess,
jumping in a Carnival Band. What did I think I
would find there? Birds in trees made present
their calls, which I at first mistook for laughter.

Q: Where are you from originally?
A: Who can speak the proper names of the dead?

In another country, I found myself
in the courtyard of a church, staring up
into the limbs of a walnut tree,
having been driven the day
past cypresses and olive groves.

Q: But how did you come to be here?
A: As we all do. I arrived a fat bundle of shit, piss,
and creaminess, unfit for this world.

In the distance I saw Nigüelas,
town of white-washed houses
crooked into mountains,
and I confessed
with such certainty I almost believed myself:
I will go there to live.

Q: I meant: How did you arrive in this country?
A: I walked into the Atlantic, as later in life
I would the Pacific and later still the Mediterranean,
each time thinking: *It's colder than the Caribbean.*

On wherever I lay my gaze
sunlight congeals in the drawing room of childhood.
Light tumbles through louvres,
                          dust motes settle on wood.

Q: Why do you keep returning to the past?
A: When I was a child, I liked digging in the dirt.
I didn't know what I was looking for. I was just digging.

        Now I think it would have been better
not to have wanted so much,

                Wanty, wanty —

        not to have asked memory to act as the self's map.

                        *

When comes the night of your unmaking?

                Stories wake in us what is inconsolable,
        begin in us again our animal mewling.

She fed pigeons. It didn't matter they were dirty,
street birds, not tidy and pretty sing-song ones
like those in abundance where I live, chickadees
and wrens and finches flitting from mulberry to
maple to dogwood. She had no trees in her yard.
Instead, Chattahoochee, paved-over grass and
flowers she grew in delineated beds and oversized
pots — roses, hibiscus, gardenia, plumbago — around
which she scattered seeds. She was at the end alone
in this house. Walking through my life far away, I
would think this: *she is alone* buying groceries *she
is alone* drinking coffee *she is alone* would tell
myself *I am not with her can't be but soon* making
dinner *next month* putting children to bed *next* —

If you listen, every word will tell you a story.
Breath
will conjure that room,
the oxygen machine compressing,

Q: I'm sorry but I have to ask this:
Are you interested in being happy?

my voice raggedly
stitching a one-way conversation,

A: When I was a young child, I wrote a poem:
I wonder how high heaven is.
I try to fly up to the sky,
but down I fall again. Plop. Plop.
Q: Okay, but that was long ago.

and her last jagged intakes of air.

A: Is this a question?

In Port-of-Spain, I had the taxi driver take me
to the address. But of course the house had been
torn down, the space where it stood an empty
lot of rockstone and weeds. This was the house
she'd slept in as a child, as if under the heaving
ribs of the whale, inside that great story of faith
at bedtime she had passed on. What now was I
to do with this tale?

*

When comes the night that made you?

Q: Shouldn't the death of ten thousand matter
more to you than that of just one person?

A: Yes. But I'm afraid grief isn't math.

                    In her story, she walked
          as if a spoke on a wheel's axis.

Q: This woman you keep speaking of, who is she?
A: Whenever I see a stream, I think *river*,
then *sea*, then *ocean*.

             She misplaced some of her children,
      two husbands, five countries, three continents.

A sudden rainfall began as the taxi drove up
the winding hill to the Abbey of Our Lady of Exile,
rain moving across the Caroni Plain like a
pen scribbling across a page. Then quickly
as it had started it stopped, and when I stepped
into the nave of the church someone
was lighting a candle, someone was murmuring.

            These were some of the facts,
      but hers, like all stories, haunts us
                not for its accuracy
          but for the promise it failed to keep:

Later, I stepped out of the church
overlooking the again sunlit plain.

          a more heroic version of the self,
               existing elsewhere.

At the end of rain there lingered
in the leaves the sound of rain.

                    *

When comes the night of your unmaking?

> *The thing I should tell she* – no,
> that's Trini and the wrong tense.
> Let me begin again:
> *The thing mi wish mi coulda tell her now* –

So it came to pass the woman grew roses.
They flourished in the garden surrounding
the house and, when clipped and arranged
in vases, filled its rooms. When the time
came to leave, of course she could not bring
them with her. Is this a story of loss or
redemption? You have to choose.

Q: Why do you make the past a fiction?
A: Everything is a wager.

> *Duppy know who to frighten.*
> I heard this as admonishment
> when a child. But now
> I think she is, I will be,
> we have all always been
> the duppy we fear.

Q: What do you mean "a wager"?
A: I needed to enact a search, but something happened
I didn't mean to have happen. I've become
a sifter and counter of grains.

> When as a child I couldn't sleep,
> stroking my arm,
> she would sit with me, repeating,

> *Two little blackbirds sitting on a wall.*
> *One name Peter. One name Paul.*

Fly away Peter. Fly away Paul.
Come back Peter. Come back Paul.

nursery rhymes, songs, nothing making sense

Round and round the garden goes the teddy bear —

but her voice and the dark.

A: I don't know where she ends and I begin.

*

When comes the night that made you?

So it also came to pass that the woman who
grew roses, fashioning a life from this rhythm
of tending, saw night fall and knew this one
would not lift. As all of this was foreseen
from the beginning, the question remains: Why
did she plant the roses in the first place?

Q: Why do you keep referring to this woman
in the third person? She is you after all, isn't she?
A: I've come to believe all stories
are self-referential. Or else none of them are.

When comes the night of your unmaking?

When as a child words found me,

Say *bird* and it will trill or twitter or even sing,
say *bird* it will fly or roost or nest, it will dig
in the dirt for worms or break open with its beak
seeds or become a plurality of one, John Crows
gathering as a single battalion into the tree.

without understanding I spoke:

Say *bird* and it will become a pair, these two
cast in frosted glass, sitting now on your dresser,
these kissing birds, these lovebirds you nagged her
soulcase for when you were a child, these birds
that rested on the coffee table in her drawing room,
these birds you wanted so desperately to have
and now you have.

Granny, when yu dead I can have these birds?

ABOUT THE AUTHOR

Shara McCallum is the author of four previous books of poetry: *The Face of Water: New and Selected Poems*, *This Strange Land*, *Song of Thieves*, and *The Water Between Us*.

Her poems have appeared in journals and magazines in the US, the Caribbean, Latin America, the UK and other parts of Europe, and Israel; have been reprinted in anthologies and textbooks of American, African American, Caribbean, and world literatures; and have been translated into Dutch, French, Italian, Romanian, and Spanish. McCallum's personal essays appear in *The Antioch Review, Creative Nonfiction, Witness,* and elsewhere.

Recognition for her work includes a Witter Bynner Fellowship from the Library of Congress, a National Endowment for the Arts Poetry Fellowship, a Walter E. Dakin Fellowship from the Sewanee Writers' Conference, a Tennessee Arts Commission Individual Artist Grant, a Cave Canem Fellowship, inclusion in the *Best American Poetry* series, and a poetry prize from the Academy of American Poets.

Originally from Jamaica, she lives with her family in Pennsylvania where she is Director of the Stadler Center for Poetry and the Margaret Hollinshead Ley Professor of Poetry & Creative Writing at Bucknell University.

ALSO BY SHARA McCALLUM

The Face of Water: New and Selected Poems
ISBN: 9781845231866; pp. 140; pub. 2011; price £9.99

Since the publication of her first collection, *The Water Between Us*, Shara McCallum has steadily created a rich body of poems that have mined the rich deposit of emotional and intellectual capital found in her background of multiple migrations, culturally and geographically.

McCallum's poems reflect her rooting in a Jamaican experience unique for her childhood in a Rastafarian home filled with reckless idealism, the potential for profound emotional pathology, and the grounding of old folks traditions. Her work has explored what it means to emerge from such a space and enter a new world of American landscapes and values. *The Face of Water* collects some of Shara Mccallum's best poems, poems that establish her as a poet of deft craft (and craftiness), whose sense of music is caught in her mastery of syntax and her ear for the graceful line. She manages in these poems to enact the grand alchemy of the best poems – the art of transforming the most painful and sometimes mundane details of life into works of terrible and satisfying beauty. McCallum demonstrates eloquently her debt to the poetics of the Caribbean and of North America, even as she establishes herself as a vital voice in the later tradition of poetry written in mutable language, English. As poet she feels no hesitation about turning that language into a very personal music. *The Face of Water* is an excellent introduction to the poetry of Shara McCallum, a vital and exciting poet of pure elegance.

This and over 340 Caribbean and Black British titles available on-line with safe ordering from www.peepaltreepress.com, by email from orders@peepaltreepress.com, by mail from Peepal Tree Press, 17 Kings Avenue, Leeds LS6 1QS, UK, or phone +44 (0)113 245 1703.